Safety
Enjoyment

by
George Cutting
(1834-1934)

1880
Gospel Folio Press
Grand Rapids, Michigan

Hope. Inspiration. Trust.

We're Social! Follow Us for New Titles and Deals:
FaceBook.com/CrossReachPublications
Twitter Handle: @CrossReachPub

Available In Paperback And eBook Editions
Please go online for More Great Titles
Available Through CrossReach Publications.
And If You Enjoyed This Book Please Consider Leaving A
Review on Amazon. That Helps Us Out A Lot. Thanks.

© 2018 CrossReach Publications
All Rights Reserved, Including The Right To Reproduce
This Book Or Portions Thereof In Any Form Whatever.

CONTENTS

"In Which Class Are You Travelling?" 5

Uncertainty 7

The Way of Salvation 9

Do You Believe on the Son of God? 12

The Knowledge of Salvation 13

The Joy of Salvation 24

About CrossReach Publications 33

Bestselling Titles from CrossReach 34

Safety, Certainty and Enjoyment

"In Which Class Are You Travelling?"

What a common question! Let me put it to you. You most certainly are travelling from time into eternity, and who knows how very, very near you may be this moment to the great terminus?

"Which class are you travelling?" There are only three. Let me describe them so you may put yourself to the test in the presence of "Him with whom we have to do."

1st Class: Those who are saved and who know it.

2nd Class: Those who are unsure of salvation, but are eager to be sure.

3rd Class: Those who are unsaved and totally indifferent about it.

Again I repeat my question: "Which class are you travelling?" Oh, the madness of indifference, when eternal issues are at stake! A short time ago, a man came rushing into the train station, and, barely

Safety, Certainty and Enjoyment

able to gasp for breath, he took his seat in one of the cars just about to start.

"You've run it close," said a fellow-passenger.

"Yes," he replied, breathing heavily after every two or three words, "but I've saved four hours, and that's well worth running for."

"Saved four hours!" I couldn't help repeating to myself, "Four hours well worth that struggle! What of eternity? What of eternity?" Yet are there not thousands of shrewd, far-seeing men today who take good care of their own interests in this life, but who are blind to the eternity before them? In spite of the infinite love of God to helpless rebels, in spite of His pronounced hatred of sin, in spite of the brevity of man's life here, in spite of the terrors of judgment after death and of the solemn probability of waking up with the unbearable remorse of being on hell's side of a "fixed" gulf, man hurries on to the bitter end, as careless as if there were no God, no death, no judgment, no heaven, no hell. If you are like that, may God this very moment have mercy upon you and open your eyes to your most perilous position, standing as you may be on a slippery brink of an endless horror.

George Cutting

Believe it or not, your case is desperate. Put off the thought of eternity no longer. Remember that procrastination is not only a "thief," but a "murderer." There is truth in the Spanish proverb which says, "The road of 'By-and-By' leads to the town of 'Never.' " I beg you, get off that road. "Now is the day of salvation."

Uncertainty

But, says one, I am not indifferent as to the welfare of my soul. My deep trouble lies wrapped up in another word — uncertainty. I am among the second-class passengers you speak of.

Well, both indifference and uncertainty are the children of one parent — unbelief. The first results from unbelief as to the sin and ruin of man, the other from unbelief as to God's sovereign remedy for man. It is especially for souls desiring before God to be fully and unmistakably sure of their salvation that these pages are written. I can, in a great measure, understand your deep soul trouble, and I am assured that the more you are in earnest about this all-important matter, the greater will be your thirst, until you know for certain that you are really and eternally saved. "What shall it profit a man, if he gain the whole world and lose his own soul?"

Safety, Certainty and Enjoyment

The only son of a devoted father is at sea. News comes that his ship has been wrecked on some foreign shore. Who can tell the anguish of suspense in that father's heart until, upon the most reliable authority, he is assured that his boy is safe and sound. Or, again, you are far from home. The night is dark and wintry, and your way is totally unknown. Standing at a point where two roads diverge, you ask a passer-by the way to the town you desire to reach, and he tells you he thinks such and such a way is the right one and he hopes you will be all right if you take it. Would "thinks" and "hopes" and "maybes" satisfy you? Surely not. You must have certainty about it, or every step you take will increase your anxiety. What wonder, then, that men have sometimes been able neither to eat nor sleep when the eternal safety of the soul has been trembling in the balance!

> To lose your wealth is much;
> To lose your health is more;
> To lose your soul is such a loss
> as no man can restore.

Now, there are three things I desire, by the Holy Spirit's help, to make clear to you, and to put them in scriptural language, they are:

1. "The way of salvation" (Acts 16:17).
2. "The knowledge of salvation" (Luke 1:77).

3. "The joy of…salvation" (Psa. 51:12).

It is quite possible for a soul to know the way of salvation without having the certain knowledge that he himself is saved, or to know that he is saved, without possessing at all times the joy that ought to accompany that knowledge.

THE WAY OF SALVATION

Please open your Bible and read carefully Exodus 13:13. There you find these words from the lips of Jehovah: "Every firstling of an ass thou shalt redeem with a lamb; and if thou wilt not redeem it, then thou shalt break his neck: and all the firstborn of man among thy children shalt thou redeem."

Now, come back with me, in thought, to a supposed scene of three thousand years ago. Two men (a priest of God and a poor Israelite) stand in earnest conversation. Let us stand by, with their permission, to listen. The gestures of each bespeak deep earnestness about some matter of importance, and it isn't difficult to see that the subject of conversation is a little ass that stands trembling beside them.

"I have come to know," says the poor Israelite, "if there cannot be a merciful exception made in my favor this once. This feeble little thing is the firstling of my ass, and though I know full well what the law of God says about it, I am hoping that mercy will be shown and the ass's life spared. I am but a poor man in Israel and can ill afford to lose the little colt."

"But," answers the priest, firmly, "the law of the Lord is plain and unmistakable. 'Every firstling of an ass thou shalt redeem with a lamb: and if thou wilt not redeem it, then thou shalt break his neck.' Where is the lamb?"

"Ah, sir, I do not have a lamb."

"Then go purchase one and return, or the ass's neck must surely be broken. The lamb must die or the ass must die."

"Alas! then all my hopes are crushed," he cries, "for I am far too poor to buy a lamb."

While this conversation proceeds, a third person joins them, and after hearing the poor man's tale of sorrow, he turns to him and says kindly, "Be of good cheer; I can meet your need." And he proceeds: "We have in our house on the hilltop yonder one little lamb brought up at our very hearthstone, who is 'without spot or blemish.' It has never once strayed from home, and it stands (and rightly so) in highest favour with all that are in the house. I will fetch it." And away he hurries up the hill. Soon you see him gently leading the little lamb down the slope, and very soon both lamb and ass are standing side by side.

Then the lamb is bound to the altar, its blood is shed, and the fire consumes it. The righteous priest now turns to the poor man and says, "You can freely take home your little colt in safety — no broken neck for it now. The lamb has died in the ass's stead and consequently the ass goes righteously free, thanks to your friend."

Can't you see in this God's own picture of a sinner's salvation? His claims as to sin demanded a "broken neck," that is, righteous judgment upon your guilty head, the only alternative being the death of a divinely approved substitute.

Now, you could not find the provision to meet your case, but, in the person of His beloved Son, God Himself provided the Lamb. "Behold the Lamb of God," said John to his disciples, as his eyes fell upon that blessed spotless One. "Behold the Lamb of God, which taketh away the sin of the world" (John 1:29).

He went to Calvary, "as a lamb to the slaughter," and there and then He "once suffered for sins, the just for the unjust, that He might bring us to God" (1 Peter 3:18). He "was delivered for our offences, and was raised again for our justification" (Rom. 4:25). God does not lower His righteous, holy claims against sin when He justifies (clears from all charge of guilt) the ungodly sinner who believes in Jesus (Rom. 3:26). Blessed be God for such a Saviour, such a salvation!

Do You Believe on the Son of God?

Well, you reply, I have, as a poor, condemned sinner, found in Him one that I can safely trust. I do believe on Him. Then I tell you, the full value of His sacrifice and death, as God estimates it, He makes as good to you as though you had accomplished it all yourself.

Oh, what a wondrous way of salvation is this! Is it not great and grand and Godlike — worthy of God Himself? The gratification of His own heart of love, the glory of His precious Son, and the salvation of a sinner are all bound up together. What a bundle of grace and glory! Blessed be the God and Father of our Lord Jesus Christ, who has so ordered it that His own beloved Son should do all the work and get all the praise, and that guilty you and I, believing on Him, should not only get all the blessings, but enjoy the blissful company of the Blesser forever. "O magnify the Lord with me, and let us exalt His name together" (Psa. 34:3).

But perhaps your eager inquiry may be, "How is it that since I do really distrust self and self-work, I have not the full certainty of my salvation?" You say, "If my feelings warrant me saying that I am saved one day, they are pretty sure to blight every hope the next, and I am left like a storm-tossed ship, without any anchorage whatever." There lies your mistake. Did you ever hear of a captain trying to find anchorage by fastening his anchor inside the ship? Never. Always outside.

It may be that you are clear that it is only Christ's death that gives safety, but you think that it is what you feel that gives certainty.

THE KNOWLEDGE OF SALVATION

Before you turn to the verse which I shall ask you very carefully to look at, which speaks of how a believer is to know that he has eternal life, let me quote it in the distorted way that man's imagination often puts it. "These happy feelings have I given unto you that believe on the name of the Son of God; that ye may know that ye have eternal life." Now, open your Bible, and while you compare this with God's blessed and unchanging Word, may He give you from your very heart to say with David, "I hate vain thoughts: but Thy law do I love" (Psa. 119:113). The verse just misquoted is 1 John 5:13, and it reads thus in our version: "These things have I written unto you that believe on the name of the Son of God; that ye may know that ye have eternal life."

How did the firstborn sons of Israel know for certain that they were safe the night of the Passover and Egypt's judgment? Let us take a visit to two of their houses and hear what they have to say.

We find in the first house we enter that they are all shivering with fear and suspense. We inquire, "What is the secret of all this paleness and trembling?" The firstborn son informs us that the angel of death is coming around the land and that he is not quite certain how matters will stand with him at that solemn moment.

"When the destroying angel has passed our house," says he, "and the night of judgment is over, I shall then know that I am safe, but I can't see how I can be quite sure of it until then. They say they are sure of salvation next door, but we think it very presumptuous. All I can do is to spend the long, dreary night hoping for the best."

"Well," we inquire, "but has the God of Israel not provided a way of safety for His people?"

"True," he replies, "and we have availed ourselves of that way of escape. The blood of the spotless and unblemished first-year lamb has been duly sprinkled with the bunch of hyssop on the lintel and two side-posts, but still we are not fully assured of shelter."

Let us now enter next door. What a striking contrast meets our eye at once! Joy shows on every face. There they stand with girded loins and staff in hand, enjoying the roasted lamb.

What can be the meaning of all this joy on such a solemn night as this? "Ah," say they all, "we are only waiting for Jehovah's marching orders and then we shall bid a last farewell to the taskmaster's cruel lash and all the drudgery of Egypt."

"But wait. Do you forget that this is the night of Egypt's judgment?"

"We know it well, but our firstborn son is safe. The blood has been sprinkled according to the wish of our God."

"But so it has been next door," we reply, "but they are all unhappy because they are all uncertain of safety."

Safety, Certainty and Enjoyment

"Ah," responds the firstborn firmly, "but we have more than the sprinkled blood; we have the unerring word of God about it. God has said, 'When I see the blood, I will pass over you.' God rests satisfied with the blood outside, and we rest satisfied with His word inside."

The sprinkled blood makes us safe.
The written word makes us sure.

Could anything make us more safe than the sprinkled blood, or more sure than His written word? Nothing, nothing.

Now, let me ask you a question. "Which of those two houses think you was the safer?"

Do you say the second, where all were so happy? No, then you are wrong. Both are safe alike. Their safety depends upon what God thinks about the blood outside and not upon the state of their feelings inside.

If you would be sure of your own blessing, then listen not to the unstable testimony of inward emotions, but to the infallible witness of the Word of God. "Verily, verily, I say unto you, He that believeth on Me hath everlasting life."

Let me give you a simple illustration from everyday life. A certain farmer in the country, not having sufficient grass for his cattle, applies for a nice piece of pasture which he hears is to be rented near his own house. For some time he gets no answer from the landlord. One day a neighbour comes in and says, "I feel quite sure you will get that field. Don't you recollect how that last Christmas he sent you a special present and that he gave you a kind nod of recognition the other day when he drove past?" And with such like words the farmer's mind is filled with hope.

Next day another neighbour meets him, and in the course of conversation he says, "I'm afraid you will stand no chance whatever of getting that field. Another has applied for it, and he is a favourite with the owner — occasionally he visits with him," and so on. And the poor farmer's bright hopes are dashed to the ground. One day he is hoping; the next day he is full of perplexing doubts.

Soon the mailman calls, and the farmer's heart beats fast as he breaks the seal of the letter, for he sees by the handwriting that it is from the owner himself. See his face change from anxious suspense to undisguised joy as he reads and re-reads that letter.

Safety, Certainty and Enjoyment

"It's a settled thing now," exclaims he to his wife; "no more doubts and fears about it. The owner says the field is mine as long as I require it, on the most easy terms. No man's opinion matters now. His word settles it."

Now many a poor soul is in a similar condition to the troubled farmer — tossed and perplexed by the opinions of men or the thoughts and feelings of his own treacherous heart, and it is only upon receiving the Word of God as the Word of God that certainty takes the place of doubt. When God speaks, there must be certainty, whether He pronounces the damnation of the unbeliever or the salvation of the believer.

"Forever, O Lord, Thy word is settled in heaven" (Psa 119:89). To the simple-hearted believer His word settles all. "Hath He said, and shall He not do it? or hath He spoken, and shall He not make it good?" (Num. 23:19).

"I need no other argument;
I want no other plea;
It is enough that Jesus died -
And that He died for me."

The believer can add, "And that God says so."

"But how may I be sure that I have the right kind of faith?"

Well, there can be but one answer to that question, namely: Have you confidence in the right person — in the blessed Son of God?

It is not a question of the amount of your faith but the trustworthiness of the person you repose your confidence in. One man takes hold of Christ, as it were, with a drowning man's grip; another but touches the hem of His garment. But the sinner who does the former is not a bit safer than the one who does the latter. They have both made the same discovery, that while all of self is totally untrustworthy, they may safely confide in Christ, calmly rely on His word, and confidently rest in the eternal value of His finished work. That is what is meant by believing on Him. "Verily, verily, I say unto you, He that believeth on Me hath everlasting life" (John 6:47).

Make sure of it, then, that your confidence is not reposed in your works of amendment, your religious observances, your pious feelings when under religious influences, your moral training from childhood, and the like. You may have the strongest faith in any or all of these and perish everlastingly. Don't deceive yourself by any "fair show in the flesh." The feeblest faith in Christ eternally saves, while the strongest faith in anything else comes from a deceived heart — only the enemy's disguise over the pit of eternal perdition.

God, in the gospel, simply introduces to you the Lord Jesus Christ, and He says, "This is My beloved Son, in whom I am well pleased." "You may," He says, "with all confidence trust His heart, though you cannot with impunity trust your own." Blessed, thrice blessed Lord Jesus, who would not trust Thee and praise Thy name!

"I do really believe on Him," said a sad-looking soul to me one day. "But yet, when asked if I am saved, I don't like to say yes, for fear I should be telling a lie." This young woman was a butcher's daughter, in a small town in the midlands. It happened to be market day, and her father had not then returned from market. So I said, "Now suppose when your father comes home, you ask him how many sheep he bought today, and he answers, 'Ten.' After a while a man comes to the shop and says, 'How many sheep did your father buy today?' and you reply, 'I don't like to say, for fear I should be telling a lie.' " "But," said the mother (who was standing by at the time), with righteous indignation, "that would be making her father a liar."

Now, don't you see that this well-meaning young woman was virtually making Christ a liar, saying, "I do believe on the Son of God, but I don't like to say I am saved lest I should be telling a lie," when Christ Himself has said, "He that believeth on Me hath everlasting life" (John 6:47)? "But," says another, "how may I be sure that I really do believe? I have tried often to believe and looked within to see if I had got it, but the more I look at my faith, the less I seem to have."

You are looking in the wrong direction to find that out, and your trying to believe but plainly shows that you are on the wrong track.

Let me give you another illustration to explain what I want to convey to you. You are sitting at your quiet fireside one evening, when a man comes in and tells you that the stationmaster has been killed that night at the railway.

Now it happens that this man has long had the reputation for being a very dishonest man and the most daring liar in the neighbourhood.

"Do you believe, or even try to believe that man?"

"Of course not," you exclaim.

"Why?"

Safety, Certainty and Enjoyment

"Oh I know him too well for that."

"But tell me how you know that you don't believe him? Is it by looking within at your faith or feelings?"

"No," you reply. "I think of the man that brings me the message."

Soon, a neighbour drops in and says, "The stationmaster has been run over by a freight train tonight and killed on the spot." After he has left, I hear you cautiously say, "Well, I partly believe it now, for, to my recollection, this man only once in his life deceived me, though I have known him from boyhood."

"But again," I ask, "is it by looking at your faith this time that you know you partly believe it?"

"No," you repeat. "I am thinking of the character of my informant."

Well, this man has scarcely left your room before a third person enters and brings you the same sad news as the first. But this time you say, "Now, John, since you tell me, I believe it."

Again, I press my question (which is, remember, only the echo of your own), "How do you know that you so confidently believe your friend John?"

"Because of who and what John is," you reply. "He never has deceived me, and I don't think he ever will."

Well, then, just in the same way I know that I believe the gospel, namely, because of the One who brings me the news. "If we receive the witness of men, the witness of God is greater: for this is the witness of God which He hath testified of His Son. … He that believeth not God hath made Him a liar: because he believeth not the record that God gave of His Son" (1 John 5:9-10). "Abraham believed God, and it was counted unto him for righteousness" (Rom. 4:3).

An anxious soul once said to a servant of Christ, "Oh sir, I can't believe!" to which the preacher wisely and quietly replied, "Indeed, who is it that you can't believe?" This broke the spell. He had been looking at faith as an indescribable something that he must feel within himself in order to be sure that he was all right for heaven, whereas faith always looks outside to a living Person and His finished work and quietly listens to the testimony of a faithful God about both.

Safety, Certainty and Enjoyment

It is the outside look that brings the inside peace. When a man turns his face towards the sun, his own shadow is behind him. You cannot look at self and a glorified Christ in heaven at the same moment.

Thus we have seen that the blessed Person of God's Son wins my confidence; His finished work makes me eternally safe; God's Word about those who believe on Him makes me unalterably sure. I find in Christ and His work the way of salvation, and in the Word of God the knowledge of salvation.

But if saved, you may say, "How is it that I have such a fluctuating experience — so often losing all my joy and comfort and getting as wretched and downcast as I was before my conversion?" Well, this brings us to our third point:

The Joy of Salvation

You will find in Scripture that while you are saved by Christ's work and assured by God's Word, you are maintained in comfort and joy by the Holy Spirit who indwells every believer.

Now you must bear in mind that every saved one has still within him "the flesh," that is, the evil nature he was born with as a natural man and which, perhaps, shows itself while still a helpless infant, on his mother's lap. The Holy Spirit in the believer resists the flesh and is grieved by every activity of it in motive, word or deed. When he is walking "worthy of the Lord," the Holy Spirit will be producing in his soul His blessed fruits — such as "love, joy, peace" (Gal. 5:22). When he is walking in a carnal, worldly way, the Spirit is grieved, and these fruits are lacking in a greater or lesser measure.

Let me put it thus for you who do believe on God's Son:

Christ's work and your salvation stand or fall together.

Your walk and your enjoyment stand or fall together.

If Christ's work could break down (and, blessed be God, it never, never will), your salvation would break down with it. When your walk breaks down (and be watchful, for it may), your enjoyment will break down with it.

Thus it is said of the early disciples (Acts 9:31) that they walked "in the fear of the Lord, and in the comfort of the Holy Ghost." And again in Acts 13:52: "The disciples were filled with joy, and with the Holy Ghost." My spiritual joy will be in proportion to the spiritual character of my walk after I am saved.

Now, do you see your mistake? You have been mixing up enjoyment with your safety — two widely different things. When, through self-indulgence, loss of temper or worldliness, you grieved the Holy Spirit and lost your joy, you thought your safety was undermined. I repeat it:

Your safety hangs upon Christ's work FOR you.
Your assurance, upon God's word TO you.
Your enjoyment, upon not grieving the Holy Spirit IN you.

When, as a child of God, you do anything to grieve the Holy Spirit of God, your communion with the Father and the Son is, for the time, practically suspended, and it is only when you judge yourself and confess your sins that the joy of communion is restored.

Your child has been guilty of some misdemeanour. His face shows that something is wrong with him. Half an hour before he was enjoying a walk with you around the garden, admiring what you admired and enjoying what you enjoyed. In other words, he was in communion with you; his feelings and sympathies were in common with yours.

But now all this is changed, and as a naughty, disobedient child, he stands in the corner, the very picture of misery. Upon penitent confession of his wrongdoing, you have assured him of forgiveness, but his pride and self-will keep him sobbing there. Where is the joy of half an hour ago? All gone. Why? Because communion between you and him has been interrupted. What has become of the relationship that existed between you and your son half an hour ago? Has that gone too? Is that severed or interrupted? Surely not. His relationship depends upon his birth; his communion, upon his behaviour.

Soon he comes out of the corner with broken will and broken heart, confessing the whole thing from first to last, so that you see he hates the disobedience and naughtiness as much as you do, and you take him in your arms and cover him with kisses. His joy is restored because communion is restored.

When David sinned so grievously in the matter of Uriah's wife, he did not say, "Restore unto me Thy salvation," but, "Restore unto me the joy of Thy salvation" (Psa 51:12).

Safety, Certainty and Enjoyment

But to carry our illustration a little farther: Supposing while your child is in the corner, there should be a cry of "House on fire!" throughout your house, what would become of him then? Left in the corner to be consumed with the burning, falling house? Impossible. Very probably he would be the very first person you would carry out. Yes, you know right well that the love of relationship is one thing, and the joy of communion quite another.

Now, when the believer sins, communion is interrupted and joy is lost until, with a broken heart, he comes to the Father in self-judgment, confessing his sins. Then he knows he is forgiven, for His Word plainly declares that "if we confess our sins, He is faithful and just to forgive us our sins, and to cleanse us from all unrighteousness" (1 John 1:9).

Dear child of God, always bear in mind these two things, that there is nothing so strong as the link of relationship and nothing so delicate as the link of communion. All the combined power and counsel of earth and hell cannot sever the former, while an impure motive or an idle word will break the latter. If you are troubled with a cloudy half hour, get low before God, consider your ways, and when the cause that has robbed you of your joy has been detected, bring it at once to the light, confess your sin to God your Father, and judge yourself most unsparingly for the careless state of soul that allowed the thief to enter unchallenged.

But never, never, never confound your safety with your joy.

Don't imagine, however, that the judgment of God falls the slightest bit more leniently on the believer's sin than on the unbeliever's. He does have two ways of dealing judicially with sin, and He could no more pass by the believer's sin without judging it than He could pass by the sins of a rejecter of His precious Son. But there is this great difference between the two, namely that the believer's sins were all known to God and all laid upon His own provided Lamb when He hung upon the cross at Calvary and that there and then, once and forever, the great "criminal question" of his guilt was raised and settled — judgment falling upon the blessed Substitute in the believer's stead, "who His own self bare our sins in His own body on the tree" (1 Peter 2:24).

The Christ-rejecter must bear his own sins in his own person in the lake of fire forever. Now, when a saved one fails, the "criminal question" of sin cannot be raised against him, the Judge Himself having settled that once for all on the cross, but the communion question is raised within him by the Holy Spirit as often as he grieves the Spirit.

Allow me, in conclusion, to give you another illustration: It is a beautiful moonlit night. The moon is full and shining in more than ordinary silvery brightness. A man is gazing intently down a deep, still well, where he sees the moon reflected, and thus remarks to a friendly bystander: "How beautifully fair and round she is tonight; how quietly and majestically she rides along!" He had just finished speaking when suddenly his friend drops a small pebble into the well and he now exclaims, "Why the moon is all broken to shivers, and the fragments are shaking together in the greatest disorder."

"What gross absurdity!" is the astonished rejoinder of his companion. "Look up, man! The moon hasn't changed in the slightest; it is the condition of the well that reflects her that has changed."

Now, believer, apply this simple figure.

Your heart is the well. When there is no allowance of evil, the blessed Spirit of God takes of the glories and preciousness of Christ and reveals them to you for your comfort and joy, but the moment a wrong motive is cherished in the heart or an idle word escapes the lips unjudged, the Holy Spirit begins to disturb the well, your happy experiences are smashed to pieces, and you are all restless and disturbed within, until, in brokenness of spirit before God, you confess your sin (the disturbing thing) and thus get restored once more to the calm, sweet joy of communion.

But when your heart is thus all unrest, need I ask, Has Christ's work changed? No, no! Then your salvation has not altered.

Has God's Word changed? Surely not. Then the certainty of your salvation has received no shock.

Then what has changed? Why, the action of the Holy Spirit in you has changed, and instead of taking the glories of Christ and filling your heart with the sense of His worthiness, He is grieved at having to turn aside from this delightful office to fill you with the sense of your sin and unworthiness.

He takes from you your present comfort and joy until you judge and resist the evil thing that He judges and resists. When this is done, communion with God has again been restored.

The Lord make us to be increasingly jealous over ourselves, lest we "grieve…the Holy Spirit of God, whereby [we] are sealed unto the day of redemption" (Eph. 4:30).

However weak your faith may be, rest assured of this, that the blessed One who has won your confidence will never change. "Jesus Christ the same yesterday, and today, and forever" (Heb. 13:8).

The work He has accomplished will never change. "Whatsoever God doeth, it shall be forever: nothing can be put to it, nor anything taken from it" (Eccl. 3:14).

The word He has spoken will never change. Thus the object of my trust, the foundation of my safety, and the ground of my certainty are alike eternally unalterable.

Once more let me ask, in which class are you travelling? Turn your heart to God and answer that question to Him. "Let God be true, but every man a liar" (Rom. 3:4).

ABOUT CROSSREACH PUBLICATIONS

Thank you for choosing CrossReach Publications.

Trust. Inspiration. Hope.

These three words sum up the philosophy of why CrossReach Publications exist. You want solid Christian books from respected and acknowledged Christian writers from yesteryear. We want to provide them for you.

Not only do you get the works of the most well-known men and women of Christendom, we have also brought back many lesser-known works from some of the giants from Church history, as well as hidden gems from less popular, and even almost forgotten authors that deserve to be heard again.

Not only that, our editions are also high quality. We spend time editing and formatting and looking over our manuscripts before publishing. Some small publishers of classic works publish sloppy, almost illegible reproductions of these works. This will not do. We aspire to excellence and we believe it shows in our editions. We cannot guarantee perfection, but we'll try. And we do this at a cost that is right for you.

If you have any questions or comments about our publications contact us:

ContactUs@CrossReach.net
https://www.CrossReach.store

Don't forget you can follow us on Facebook and Twitter, (addresses are on the copyright page above) to keep up to date on our newest titles and deals.

BESTSELLING TITLES FROM CROSSREACH[1]

God Still Speaks
A. W. Tozer
$6.99
https://amazon.com/dp/154980894X

Tozer is as popular today as when he was living on the earth. He is respected right across the spectrum of Christianity, in circles that would disagree sharply with him doctrinally. Why is this? A. W. Tozer was a man who knew the voice of God. He shared this experience with every true child of God. With all those who are called by the grace of God to share in the mystical union that is possible with Him through His Son Jesus.

Tozer fought against much dryness and formality in his day. Considered a mighty man of God by most Evangelicals today, he was unconventional in his approach to spirituality and had no qualms about consulting everyone from Catholic Saints to German Protestant mystics for inspiration on how to experience God more fully.

Tozer, just like his Master, doesn't fit neatly into our theological boxes. He was a man after God's own heart

---

[1] Most of our eBooks cost between $0.99 and $1.99. Most of our paperbacks cost $7.99 or less. Click on the title of each to be brought to the eBook edition or if this is a paperback, then copy the address into your internet browser. Buy from CrossReach Publications for quality and price. We have a full selection of titles in print and eBook, available on Amazon and a growing selection of other online stores. You can see our full selection just by searching for CrossReach Publications in the search bar of these stores!

and was willing to break the rules (man-made ones that is) to get there.

Here are two writings by Tozer that touch on the heart of this goal. Revelation is Not Enough and The Speaking Voice. A bonus chapter The Menace of the Religious Movie is included.

This is meat to sink your spiritual teeth into. Tozer's writings will show you the way to satisfy your spiritual hunger.

The 400 Silent Years
H. A. Ironside
$7.50
https://amazon.com/dp/1549816039

Fully illustrated. Includes all of the drawings from the original edition.

What is the history between the Old and New Testaments? Most people are not even aware there is such a gap. But there is. A 400 year gap.

When the Old Testament leaves off the Jews have just returned back from Babylonian captivity and the Persian Empire is in full swing. When Jesus enters the scene it is 400 years later. The Persians are long gone, the Greeks have had their time and now the Romans rule to roost.

So what happened? Do we have any writings from this time? Could understanding this period of time help us understand the New Testament, the world of Jesus and the Apostles? The answer is yes.

This exciting book by well-known author H. A. Ironside lifts the veil from this vital period of Jewish history and helps piece together the events that brought them from Malachi to Matthew.

This book will be of interested to students of Biblical, Ancient Near Eastern, Greek and Roman history as well as all those who desire to know and understand the Bible for fully.

Christianity and Liberalism
J. Gresham Machen

The purpose of this book is not to decide the religious issue of the present day, but merely to present the issue as sharply and clearly as possible, in order that the reader may be aided in deciding it for himself. Presenting an issue sharply is indeed by no means a popular business at the present time; there are many who prefer to fight their intellectual battles in what Dr. Francis L. Patton has aptly called a "condition of low visibility." Clear-cut definition of terms in religious matters, bold facing of the logical implications of religious views, is by many persons regarded as an impious proceeding. May it not discourage contribution to mission boards? May it not hinder the progress of consolidation, and produce a poor showing in columns of Church statistics? But with such persons we cannot possibly bring ourselves to agree. Light may seem at times to be an impertinent intruder, but it is always beneficial in the end. The type of religion which rejoices in the pious sound of traditional phrases, regardless of their meanings, or shrinks from "controversial" matters, will never stand amid the shocks of life. In the sphere of religion, as in other spheres, the things about which men are agreed are apt to be the things that are least worth holding; the really important things are the things about which men will fight.

How to Be Filled with the Holy Spirit

A. W. Tozer
$6.99
https://amazon.com/dp/1549774190

Before we deal with the question of how to be filled with the Holy Spirit, there are some matters which first have to be settled. As believers you have to get them out of the way, and right here is where the difficulty arises. I have been afraid that my listeners might have gotten the idea somewhere that I had a how-to-be-filled-with-the-Spirit-in-five-easy-lessons doctrine, which I could give you. If you can have any such vague ideas as that, I can only stand before you and say, "I am sorry"; because it isn't true; I can't give you such a course. There are some things, I say, that you have to get out of the way, settled.

The Two Babylons

Alexander Hislop
$7.99
https://amazon.com/dp/1549771191

Fully Illustrated High Res. Images. Complete and Unabridged.

Expanded Seventh Edition. This is the first and only seventh edition available in a modern digital edition. Nothing is left out! New material not found in the first six editions!!! Available in eBook and paperback edition exclusively from CrossReach Publications.

"In his work on "The Two Babylons" Dr. Hislop has proven conclusively that all the idolatrous systems of the nations had their origin in what was founded by that mighty Rebel, the beginning of whose kingdom was Babel (Gen. 10:10)."—A. W. Pink, The Antichrist (1923)

There is this great difference between the works of men and the works of God, that the same minute and searching investigation, which displays the defects and imperfections of the one, brings out also the beauties of the other. If the most finely polished needle on which the art of man has been expended be subjected to a microscope, many inequalities, much roughness and clumsiness, will be seen. But if the microscope be brought to bear on the flowers of the field, no such result appears. Instead of their beauty diminishing, new beauties and still more delicate, that have escaped the naked eye, are forthwith discovered; beauties that make us appreciate, in a way which otherwise we could have had little conception of, the full force of the Lord's saying, "Consider the lilies of the field, how they grow; they toil not, neither do they spin: and yet I say unto you, That even Solomon, in all his glory, was not arrayed like one of these." The same law appears also in comparing the Word of God and the most finished productions of men. There are spots and blemishes in the most admired productions of human genius. But the more the Scriptures are searched, the more minutely they are studied, the more their perfection appears; new beauties are brought into light every day; and the discoveries of science, the researches of the learned, and the labours of infidels, all alike conspire to illustrate the wonderful harmony of all the parts, and the Divine beauty that clothes the whole. If this be the case with Scripture in general, it is especially the case with prophetic Scripture. As every spoke in the wheel of Providence revolves, the prophetic symbols start into still more bold and beautiful relief. This is very strikingly the case with the prophetic language that forms the groundwork and corner-stone of the present work. There never has been any difficulty in the mind of any enlightened Protestant in identifying the woman "sitting on seven mountains," and having on her forehead the name written, "Mystery, Babylon the Great," with the Roman apostacy.

What We Are In Christ
E. W. Kenyon
$5.99
https://amazon.com/dp/1549823094

I was surprised to find that the expressions "in Christ," "in whom," and "in Him" occur more than 130 times in the New Testament. This is the heart of the Revelation of Redemption given to Paul.

Here is the secret of faith—faith that conquers, faith that moves mountains. Here is the secret of the Spirit's guiding us into all reality. The heart craves intimacy with the Lord Jesus and with the Father. This craving can now be satisfied.

Ephesians 1:7: "In whom we have our redemption through his blood, the remission of our trespasses according to the riches of his grace."

It is not a beggarly Redemption, but a real liberty in Christ that we have now. It is a Redemption by the God Who could say, "Let there be lights in the firmament of heaven," and cause the whole starry heavens to leap into being in a single instant. It is Omnipotence beyond human reason. This is where philosophy has never left a footprint.

The Complete Wycliffe Bible: Old Testament, New Testament & Apocrypha: Text Edition
$18.99
https://amazon.com/dp/154978692X

In making this edition of Wycliffe's monumental work the Publisher has had to make a number of decisions that affect the final outcome of the work. Some of these decisions may be welcomed by the reading public and some perhaps not. All of the decisions were made with the reader in mind. Our intention was to produce an edition of Wycliffe's Bible translation that was reasonably priced and to do this it must be in one volume. This has meant choosing a large paper format. Other smaller sized editions are over 800 pages. We chose a larger paper size that results in around 250 pages less. We chose a font that is recognized as easily readable at smaller sizes. Adobe Garamond, 10 pt. was selected. We have tested it and have not found it to be an uncomfortable reading size. If you have reasonable eyesight, you will not need a magnifying glass, as has been reportedly needed for other modern reprints. We hope you like it. Some will complain that we have not inserted indents and paragraphing. Again, this is a massive volume and we have tried to produce a book that is within one volume so that it is commercially viable for us and you the reader. It has also meant not including any of the introductions by Wycliffe, Jerome and others, or notes that were a part of the original. Hence the subtitle "Text Edition". We understand this will not be to everyone's liking, but we are limited, by the printer, to how many pages our books can be. At the size we chose we are almost at capacity. At a smaller size we could have done over 800 pages, but we still would have had to cram the same amount of text in. So the problem would be the same. The only way around this problem would have been to produce two large volumes and at this time we do question the viability of such an undertaking. However, if it is clear that there is a great demand for it, we may bring out a new two volume edition with that additional text. This work was first produced in the late Middle Ages. The language is therefore extremely archaic. So much so that some of the letters have evolved and changed since then. This edition contains all modern letters, but does not contain modern spelling. It is therefore, not a "Modern Edition" in this sense. The yogh for example has been replaced as necessary. Purists will complain, but we hope for the average reader this will not present much of a problem. It will hopefully give the reader a text as close to the original yet still possible to be read and, with a little work, understood.

How to Prepare Sermons
William Evans
$7.99
https://amazon.com/dp/154981785X

This volume is not an attempt to present a complete and exhaustive treatment on Homiletics—the science and art of preaching, for there are already on the market larger and more comprehensive works on the subject. This book is prepared not only for theological students but also to supply the need of such as find themselves denied the privileges of a regular ministerial training, but who, nevertheless, feel themselves called upon to preach or proclaim the gospel of the Lord Jesus Christ. Indeed the lectures herein printed are in substance the same as delivered to young men and women preparing themselves for Christian service in a Bible training school. This fact accounts for their conversational style, which the author has not deemed wise to change. Christian laymen, even though not preachers in the accepted sense of that term, desiring to be able to prepare brief gospel addresses and Bible readings, will find the help they need in this volume. Those seeking help in the preparation of "talks" for young peoples' societies, conventions, leagues, etc., may receive hints and suggestions in this work. The book contains theory and practice. Part One deals with the method of constructing various kinds of sermons and Bible addresses. Part Two is composed of outlines illustrating Part One. The closing chapter on "Illustrations and Their Use" has been found so helpful wherever delivered that it is thought advisable to give it a place in this volume.

Claiming Our Rights
E. W. Kenyon
$7.99
www.amazon.com/dp/1549815148

There is no excuse for the spiritual weakness and poverty of the Family of God when the wealth of Grace and Love of our great Father with His power and wisdom are all at our disposal. We are not coming to the Father as a tramp coming to the door begging for food; we come as sons not only claiming our legal rights but claiming the natural rights of a child that is begotten in love. No one can hinder us or question our right of approach to our Father.

Satan has Legal Rights over the sinner that God cannot dispute or challenge. He can sell them as slaves; he owns them, body, soul and spirit. But the moment we are born again... receive Eternal Life, the nature of God,—his legal dominion ends.

Christ is the Legal Head of the New Creation, or Family of God, and all the Authority that was given Him, He has given us: (Matthew 28:18), "All authority in heaven," the seat of authority, and "on earth," the place of execution of authority. He is "head over all things," the highest authority in the Universe, for the benefit of the Church which is His body.

The Person and Work of the Holy Spirit
R. A. Torrey
$5.85
www.amazon.com/dp/1549821490

Before one can correctly understand the work of the Holy Spirit, he must first of all know the Spirit Himself. A frequent source of error and fanaticism about the work of the Holy Spirit is the attempt to study and understand His work without first of all coming to know Him as a Person.

It is of the highest importance from the standpoint of worship that we decide whether the Holy Spirit is a Divine Person, worthy to receive our adoration, our faith, our love, and our entire surrender to Himself, or whether it is simply an influence emanating from God or a power or an illumination that God imparts to us. If the Holy Spirit is a person, and a Divine Person, and we do not know Him as such, then we are robbing a Divine Being of the worship and the faith and the love and the surrender to Himself which are His due.

Home Geography for the Primary Grades
C. C. Long
$7.95
https://amazon.com/dp/1518780660

A popular homeschooling resource for many generations now. Geography may be divided into the geography of the home and the geography of the world at large. A knowledge of the home must be obtained by direct observation; of the rest of the world, through the imagination assisted by information. Ideas acquired by direct observation form a basis for imagining those things which are distant and unknown. The first work, then, in geographical instruction, is to study that small part of the earth's surface lying just at our doors. All around are illustrations of lake and river, upland and lowland, slope and valley. These forms must be actually observed by the pupil, mental pictures obtained, in order that he may be enabled to build up in his mind other mental pictures of similar unseen forms. The hill that he climbs each day may, by an appeal to his imagination, represent to him the lofty Andes or the Alps. From the meadow, or the bit of level land near the door, may be developed a notion of plain and prairie. The little stream that flows past the schoolhouse door, or even one formed by the sudden shower, may speak to him of the Mississippi, the Amazon, or the Rhine. Similarly, the idea of sea or ocean may be deduced from that of pond or lake. Thus, after the pupil has acquired elementary ideas by actual perception, the imagination can use them in constructing, on a larger scale, mental pictures of similar objects outside the bounds of his own experience and observation.

A Medicine Chest for Christian Practitioners
Clarence Larkin
$4.99
https://amazon.com/dp/1520411316

This booklet is designed to give tools for Christian service. Clarence Larkin was born October 28, 1850, in Chester, Delaware County, Pennsylvania. He was converted to Christ at the age of 19. He was a mechanical engineer, teacher and manufacturer by trade. In 1884, at the age of 34, he became an ordained Baptist minister. His first pastorate was at Kennett Square, Pennsylvania; his second was at Fox Chase, Pennsylvania, where he remained for 20 years. He was not a premillennialist at the time of his ordination, but his study of the Scriptures, with the help of some books that fell into his hands, led him to adopt the premillennialist position. He began to make large wall charts, which he titled, "Prophetic Truth," for use in the pulpit. These led to his being invited to teach, in connection with his pastoral work, in two Bible institutes. During this time he published a number of prophetical charts, which were widely circulated. He spent three years of his life designing and drawing the charts and preparing the text for his most noteworthy book "Dispensational Truth." Because it had a large and wide circulation in this and other lands, the first edition was soon exhausted. It was followed by a second edition, and then, realizing that the book was of permanent value, Larkin revised it and expanded it, printing it in its present form. Larkin followed this masterpiece with other books. During the last five years of his life, the demand for Larkin's books made it necessary for him to give up the pastorate and devote his full time to writing. He went to be with the Lord on January 24, 1924.—The Christian Worker's Outfit

Elementary Geography
Charlotte Mason
$8.99
https://amazon.com/dp/1549774859

This little book is confined to very simple "reading lessons upon the Form and Motions of the Earth, the Points of the Compass, the Meaning of a Map: Definitions."
It is hoped that these reading lessons may afford intelligent teaching, even in the hands of a young teacher.
Children should go through the book twice, and should, after the second reading, be able to answer any of the questions from memory.

WE OFFER A LARGE & GROWING SELECTION OF CHRISTIAN TITLES
ALL AVAILABLE THROUGH YOUR FAVOURITE ONLINE STORES
JUST SEARCH FOR CROSSREACH PUBLICATIONS!

Made in United States
North Haven, CT
19 June 2022